T0381427

PROOF of GOD

JUDAS THE LEPER DISCIPLE

Leland Cole

To order additional copies of this book, contact:
Xlibris
1-888-795-4274
www.Xlibris.com
Orders@Xlibris.com

Make Time
For God

In man's search for the truth of God, his spurning of the study of the word of God is the one visible defect that man ignores. Our apparent contempt for the things God commands against cause us to reinterpret God according to our desires. As stated in my previous book, it is my desire to reveal the truth of God not only to American Black youth, but, to all Americans. This truth is of the one true God and his love for all men which He created.

We seek Gods favor in specific areas of our life, however, we fail to realize that he has given us everything we need for all of life. This is accomplished by the spirit He has given to all men (1Cor12:7). It must be understood that the maturing of this spirit will only be accomplished by the study of Gods word.

With all the electronic media in existence today, it is very sad that for the most part, we use it not for the study of the word of God. I recall a situation where an individual was being offered an opportunity in sales and marketing. He politely declined stating he couldn't "find" the time. The salesman politely informed him that you don't "find" time, you "make" time. This is the problem with society today. We decided we want nothing to do with God to the point that anything we can fill our time with, will do. This attitude is the attitude that allows error in "understanding" of the word of God. While it is clearly evident in today's society, misinterpretation and ommission of Gods statues has continued since the beginning (Ecc1:9). It must be understood that wisdom of Gods word comes only by the study of Gods word, and, by asking Him (Jam1:5).

When we choose to do what is right in our own eyes (Jud17:6,21:25), we violate the law of God (Deut12:8) and open ourselves to the error such as committed after Solomom to Jesus and now. Because Solomon did not fully follow the Lord (1Kin11:6), God determined that the kingdom would depart from him (1Kin11:11). The kingdom was to split, with ten tribes coming under the leadership of Jeroboam (1Kin11:31).

It was this Jeroboam which committed the sin which has continued until this day. Because of his lack of trust of the word of God, he worried about losing the kingdom when the people would return to Jerusalem to worship. He "took counsel" and made two calves of gold and proclaimed to the people "behold thy gods..." (1Kin12:28). This was nearly 1000 years since the Exodus, however, there was the rememberance of the golden calf which Aaron made (Ex32:4).

It was Aaron's responsibility as the leader in worship to interpert Gods word. He, like Moses, was a Levite. This was the tribe specifically chosen by God for the position of priesthood (Num18:23). However, Jeroboam commenced the practice of allowing "whomsoever would" to be placed in the service of the priesthood. This practice was subsequently followed by many future leaders of Israel and continued through the time of Jesus. It became known as "the sins of Jeroboam". Other "sins" the people committed were to not walk according to the commandments of the Lord but "walked" according to the statutes that they themselves made (2Kin17:19).

This turning from the commands of God and instituting our own laws which contradict what God has commanded continues today.

Jeroboam made the lowest of the people priests and consecrated whosoever would (1Kin13:33). This sin was such that the house of Jeroboam was cursed to be cut off and destroyed from the face of the earth (1Kin13:34). This is the thing we continue to do today. We make statutes and laws in contradiction of Gods statutes, not realizing that God holds judgement (Ecc8:11) in order that we have time to reconsider and turn from our own way. God repeatedly warns that hell enlarges herself for all those who choose to ignore the statutes of God (Isa5:14). Today we ignore Gods statutes by instituting our own laws concerning every aspect of life, effectively disregarding Gods commandments.

The word of God repeatedly shows that a nation that has become oblivious to the statutes of God are a nation that has decided to openly declare their sin and hide it not (Isa3:9). Americans have allowed politicians to "speak villany", "practice hypocrispy, and utter error against the Lord" (Isa32:6). This also has taken place in our legal system, which, is totally based on the laws of God from the Bible. As with many areas in life, the word of God can, in many areas, be misconstrued to appear to mean this or that. However, everything in the word of God has only one meaning. Anyone with any knowledge of the Word of God knows that the direction that America is presently taking is totally contrary to the word of God.

The grace and mercy of God has made a way for us to be forgiven for the sins we as a nation commit through ignorance (Lev4:13). We Americans must understand that God "has" warned that "The vile person shall be no more called liberal,...". (Isa32:5). We are becoming a nation that has forsaken the Lord. Isiah 1:4 states, "Ah sinful nation, a people laden with iniquity, a seed of evildoers, children that are corrupters; they have forsaken the Lord, they have provoked the Holy One of Israel unto anger, they are gone away backward.". When we are not "willing and obedient" to the word of God, we will not "eat the good of the land". Our leaders will be companions of thieves, loving gifts (Isiah 1:19-23).

This appear to be the case with our present day Supreme Courts at the state and national level. The supreme courts are proving to be satans courts rather than the court of the American people. In every state where the "idea" of changing the definition of "marriage" was "voted" on, it was voted "down" by a majority. Tragically, in every state, and, nationally, there was not "one" majority of justices, o f any state, which agreed with the voice of the majority of the people of that state. When it comes to "setting Judgement" on issues, they are so secular minded that they overlook the "LAW OF JUDGEMENT" (Ex18:21). This is because those in the position of judgement have not made time for God in their life.

To overturn the voice of the people on a subject so basic could be for no other reason than the individual has not made time of God in their life. When you consider the fact that the issue of "marriage" was "legally" voted on as a republic nation "requires". A vote as designed by the Constitution, with amendments. A vote where the will of the people was in agreement with the biblical principles upon which this nation was founded. Consequencly, we Americans learned that at no level of Judgement is there a majority of Justices that agree with the people. The most shocking revelation is that there was apparently not "one" judge of either state who understood two simple terms. Particularily when they ruled, based on the fact of one simple term, "standing".

To this day I am still not sure what that's about, but, I know two terms and one takes precedent over all. You must consider that if the purpose is to redefine, in considering the answer, you consider two things. One, is what is "usual". In a "Webster American College" dictionary, "usual" is defined as "expected by reason of previous experience". I feel this in itself is suffcent to sustain the present definition of marriage once and for all. Since the justices were concerned with "standing" the second term to obviously consider is "precedent". The "precedent" is the "guideline, standard, criterion: for any and all situations of law. Precedent is "an act or instance that may serve as an example or justification for subsequent situations".

Now, I may "love" my dog, as many over the centuries has, but precedence would not allow that to be called a marriage. Based on that one "term", the justices should have "ruled" to maintain the present "definition. However, I am inclined to believe that they in someway or another received a "promise" of some sort to forego "right" judgement. Or, they were afraid of "something" other than God.

I once learned that "deciding not to decide, is a decision". If the SC justices are willing to make such a "desolate" decision concerning something with a heritage of "precedence" spanning millions of generation for the sake of one generation, I believe this is the show of the depravity that has been allowed to succeed in this generation. We have become "inventors of evil things" (Rom1:30).

Government of the People

In today's society, the American people has allowed the government and judicial system to "interpret" the Consititution in ways that violate the intent of the Constitution. The original purpose was to "...form a more perfect Union, establish Justice, insure domestic Tranquility, provide for the common defence, promote the general Welfare, and insure the Blessings of Liberty to ourselves and our Posterity,...". In order to promote these principles, the Declaration of Independence was written. The Declaration held that there were certain "Rights" endowed by the "Creator", and the Governments derived "..their just Powers from the Consent of the Governed, that whenever any Form of Government becomes destructive of these Ends, it is the Right of the People to alter or to abolish it, and institute new Governement,...".

The purpose of this reorganization of Government by the people was to construct a system "...as to them shall seem most likely to effect their Safety and Happiness.". Our present Government is filled with so-called "liberal" thinkers who have found it politically expedient to eradicate God from decisions which affect the general public. Under the liberal banner, American politicians are "legislating" morality. The American public, because of apathy, are beginning to suffer the consequences.

We are allowing our judicial system to legislate morality, calling those things, that God, our "Creator" declared in the Constitution, called evil, to now be called good (Isa5:20). All this is occuring because of the so-called liberal influence. While God recognizes true "liberal" individuals as those who devise generous or nobel things (Isa 32:8), He warns that "The vile person shall be no more called liberal,..." (Isa32:5). In society's attempt to "legalize" sin, we have completely shunned the commandments of God.

While we dismiss the present troubles as social, and not religious, there is a great social upheaval called the "Occupy" movement. I see this movement as searching for a righteous cause to effect change in society. However, in the last 50 years, American society (politicians) has been being programmed to diminish the importance of God. Because of this, faith in prayer to overcome current crises is non-existent. However, even with prayer, God always requires our action.

I recently saw a bumper sticker which read "Re-elect No One". While I feel this would be extreme, I feel such a message received by current politicians would elicit a genuine "superficial" result. However, it is the "function" of the government which should be reconsidered.

While not wanting to simplify a monumental endeavor, the solution to the present economic problems are a simple undertaking. Also with the so-called "billionars" that America has, their willingness to sacrifice as they expect the "99%" would be the beginning to returning America to a sound financial status. Once this process is begun, the revamping of the government to a form most likely to effect the "Safety and Happinesss" of all Americans can begin. This revamping would be based on a government more concerned for the welfare of its citizens.

Consider the federal budget. Total spending is divided into three categories for a total deficit of $3.83 trillion dollars. There is Mandatory spending which include Social Security ($730 billion), Medicare ($491 billion) and Medicaid ($297 billion). Also included in Mandatory spending is Troubled Asset Relief ($11 billion), Jobs initiatives ($25 billion) and OTHER ($612 billion). This total Mandatory spending comes to $2.1 trillion dollars.

The second category of the debt is Discretionary which is Defense ($895 billion) and OTHER Discretionary ($520 billion). This total spending is $1.4 trillion dollars. The final category is OTHER which is Interest on debt ($251 billion) and Potential disaster costs ($3 billion). These totals are the total American debt ($3.83 trillion).

The interesting aspect is where the money comes from. Individual income taxes ($1.1 trillion), Social Security and other payroll taxes ($934 billion) come to a total of $2.03 trillion dollars. However, the combined Corporate Income Taxes ($297 billion), Excise taxes ($74 billion), Estate and gift taxes ($25 billion), Customs duties ($27 billion) and OTHER ($87 billion) is less than $600 billion dollars. This total revenue of $257 trillion leaves a deficit of $1.27 trillion dollars. From these figures it is clear that the public is made to bear the burdeon while the hundreds of corporations raking in billions yearly contribute less than $300 billion in taxes to fund their wars. The American people must understand that the things the government attended to in the past can not continue to provide the "life, liberty and pursuit of happiness" that they provided in the past.

Our roads, while not perfect, are continuing to receive tax funds as if they had not already connected the nation. The roads as well as other similar areas has reached the point of transition that was reached when cars began to replace the horse. Blacksmiths suddenly had to become auto mechanics. Our society has reached this point on all levels. The next step is conversion from fossil to clean.

At the beginning of the present economic crises, I found it strange that the government was in a company bail out frame of mind. There were many more practical courses which the government "of the people" could take to assist our country and economy. It seems silly to even think that no one considered an economic bail out of the citizens of the nation as a viable alternative.

We as a people have created a government that has made it's citizens it's servants while taking more than one tenth of our income (1Sam8:17). If the people were to have protested this bail out for companies and opted for individual bail out, the people would have experienced the greatest benefit. This solution, however, is considered very impractical. It is assumed that the companies which have created the economic hardships plaguing the nation need the bail out in order to correct their irresponsible speculations. This bail out is not going to assist the American public. Thousands or millions will still experience economic devastation even though their present employment may be saved.

The problem with the economy are the millions unable to make payment on their multi-million dollar purchases.

Mortgage companies speculating and "dependent" upon those payments have created the economic situation facing the nation. Other companies have made expansion speculations which rising fuel costs made payment on impossible. It is called the domino effect. Because of the layoffs, the government has come to the conclusion that the bail out of the companies will solve this situation. The only conclusion the government should consider is investigating the failures and prosecuting the guilty. Also, if it were truely the government of the people, any financial bail out should be to the American public.

For instance, there are, according to the last census, there are approximately 250 million people in America. More than 50 million live in homes valued less than a million dollars.

If the government were to have given each "household" one million dollars, this would better provide the stimulus the country needed. Plus, the tax burdeon of 250 million on the nation would be considerably less than the 700 billion already approved, which, will not benefit the general public in the least. This 250 million estimate should be considered a high figure due to the fact that the "bail out" would be to households not individuals.Those able to rid themselves of mortgage payments would be in a position to stimulate the economy or provide savings income by the freed up and possibly excess stimulus income. Also, the national debt would be approximately 700 billion less. However, as stated earlier, if the 1% stepped up concerning the national debt, it could possibly be taken care of in short order.

The government response to assist companies could be to provide subsidies to companies in transition to alternative energy sources. This would include the auto industry in order to develope the technology and lower the costs of present advancements for the "average" American. Concurrently, this "household" bail out would allow most Americans to take part in the development of new alternative energy companies. Many could have "stock" in the various aspect that goes into the economical production of AE components. I believe there is no American who has not noticed that the size of cars are getting smaller while the price and gas are going up. I personally find it hard to believe that there are not electronic technologies available today to produce a viable, economic, "current trend" size car capable of internal generated power.

The government regulation on medical services would be to require and provide latest equipment to each state through taxes.

These and similar questions should be in the forefront of the "occupy" movement if they are truely concerned for the welfare of this nation. Concerns about issues such as DOMA (1Cor7:2,Lev18:22), FCC regulations (Lev5:1) and Corporate tax (loop hole) laws. Employment practices which excluded those seeking employment because of previous "encounters" with the police. This issue was recently brought to light by a lawsuit against the "Pepsi" corporation. Also, there are possibly millions of unemployed willing to work, but, afraid of a no pass drug test. Educational funding and focus must be reassesed. Lotteries are proving to not be adequate for school funding.

The reason lotteries are proving to not be adequate is possible because of the payoffs that are made somewhat legally that diminish the amounts received by the schools.

Nursing homes, abortion, hospitals and welfare are issues which funding on a state by state basis, using the property tax model of disbursement, as a means of new funding. These ideas should be in the forefront of the "occupy" movement because "Where there is no vision, the people perish:..." (Pro29:18).

God Has Final Judgement

There is a misconception in the so-called "gay" society that Christians "judge" because they voice that the gay lifestyle is wrong. I do not believe that there is a christian that hates someone who proclaim their right to be gay. Christians believe that there is a hell, and, that those who practice "unrighteousness" will not inherit the kingdom of God (1Cor4:14).

While there is considered 10 prime basic laws (the 10 Commandments), there are many other laws which were commanded. However, many are not specifically commanded in the New Testament. For example, the commandment to keep the sabboth (Ex20:8) is never given in the New Testament. However, the command against a "man lie with mankind" (Lev20:13), is (1Cor6:9).

For this reason, Christians attempt to point out that God expects us to turn from the sin that so easily beset us (Heb12:1). This pointing, should always lead to the word of God because Christians believe that the Bible is inspired by God for doctrine, reproof, correction and instruction in righteousness (2Tim3:16). The Bible is very clear that to commit "sins of the flesh" is to not inherit the kingdom of God (1Cor6:9). Christians are required to "have no company with" and admonish as a "brother" anyone who obeys not this epistle (2Thess3:14-15). This "tactic" is to induce "shame" unto repentance (Eph5:11-12). Bottom line is that most people do not seek God (Psm10:4).

However, the gay community has begun an attact on the 14th amendment in order to surcomvent the amendment with "reverse discrimination" laws cloaked as gay rights laws. Any rational individual reading the 14th amendment would see that the rights of "all" Americans is the guarentee. The laws that have gone into effect to "protect" this particular segment of society, are not only a "legal" reverse discrimination law, but, are in violation of the principles of the 14th amendment. The 14th amendment was ratified in 1868. It is since this time that the gay community has had the legal right of protection in this country. This right is the ""constitutional" right of "All persons born or naturalized" in this country.

The 14th amendment not only confers this right upon each citizen, but, prohibits individual states from "enforcing" laws which "abridge the privileges or immunities of the citizens...". This point is where the reverse discrimination comes in. The gay community is not seeking equal protection of the law. They seek to change laws to violate the moral principles upon which these laws were founded (2Kin17:9;Mal3:7). If an individual, based on their moral standard, object to a situation they find morally wrong, should they face "legal" persecution because of verbally expressed objection? This is the results of the current gay rights legislation. It provides not greater "legal protection of the law...", but "abridge the privileges and immunities..." of others.

This is somewhat the current situation with the "Boy Scouts". Because as an organization they wish to not be an organization which promote values possibly contrary to a scouts family values, they are being accused of being against these alternative lifestyles. Another American business which is experiencing this reverse discrimination because their beliefs contradict with those who wish to live contrary to the commandments and statutes of God is Chick-fil-A. The problem is that we have become a reprobate society which can not see the absurdity of the things we allow. This national attitude is why God could give our nation over to our reprobate minds to do those things that are worthy of death. (Rom1:28-32).

For instance, our society is allowing a segment to condemn the Boy Scouts for not permitting an individual with same sex tendancies to be accepted as a leader over young boys. Yet, our same society condemns Penn State University over the actions of one man with same sex tendancies!

However, we want to force this organization to accept a situation which could 15 to 20 years later come back and bite them. I think it is called "catch 22". There are times that I wonder if we are not in the "last days", however, I would have to answer "yes" and "no" to that thought. When you see the things of the Bible open up before your eyes you can only wonder. In 2 Thessalonians 2:3 it states that the day of Christ "...shall not come, except there come a falling away first, and that man of sin be revealed, the son of perdition;...".

The "important" rights that are sought are rights "any" citizen could obtain through the writing of a will or making insurance payments. This nation must understand that God is clear that, although someone may have committed sins, when they become a new creation through belief in Jesus, they no longer commit such sins "without" guilt and shame. However, today in our nation, our turning from the commandments of God has caused the words of Jesus to bear witness. "And this is the condemnation, that light`is come into the world, and men loved darkness rather than light, because their deeds were evil. (John3:19).

In Revelation 20:14 it states "And death and hell were cast into the lake of fire. This is the second death." We as humans and Christians must understand that down to the "idle word" that is spoken will be untimately judged by God. However, he that overcometh shall inherit all things (Rev20:7). This is the wonderful thing about the word of God. That it is Gods will that all men be saved (1Tim2:4). But God didn't make robots which means we have a choice to make. The sad thing is that in America today the way of truth is evil spoken of by those who wish to live contrary to the commands of God (2Pet2:2). We are doing the same things which were done in the past concerning of statutes of God (2Kin17:15). We must realize, and, stop, making laws which contradict Gods laws.

We are allowing a small segment of society to legally cast off proper moral leadership for those that "tickle the ear". Each of us as Americans must accept the truth that this country was founded by those who gave honor to God and sought His guidance in the establishment of this nation. But while God expects those that know Him to warn those who don't, I feel many Christians, myself included are more comfortable with "But if any man be ignorant, let him be ignorant (1Cor14:38)." This attitude is found in the Qur'an also in sutra 2 v6 where it states "As for those who reject faith, It is the same to them whether thou warn them or do not warn them, They will not believe.". It says "These are they who have bartered guidance for error (v16). The book of Chronicles specifically warns us about our judgements.

In 2 Chronicles 19:10 it states, "And what cause soever shall come to you of your brethren that dwell in their cities, between blood and blood, between law and commandment, statutes and judgment, ye shall even warn them that they tresspass NOT against the Lord,...". In 2 Timothy 2:19 it states that "..., The Lord knoweth them that are his. And let every one that nameth the name of Christ depart from iniquity.". We must continually remember that everyday we are confronted with choices. Some life altering, some not. For instance, to text or answer a handheld phone while driving is a choice. To believe the word of God in its truth is a choice.

To not believe the word of God is to choose death and hell instead of life. Isaiah 5:14 states, "Therefore hell hath enlarged herself, and opened her mouth without measure: and their glory, and their multitude, and their pomp, and he that rejoiceth, shall descend into it.". Hebrews 9:27 reminds us "And as it is appointed unto men once to die, but after this the judgement:...", and that all who name the name of Christ should depart from iniquity(2Tim2:19).

Judas, The Leper Disciple

The name of Judas has become synonymous with that of a betrayor or traitor. During the time of Jesus, the name Judas was a very common name. However, the man, Judas Iscariot changed all that. There are about 21 chapters in the four gospels which refer to Judas Iscariot. Just like the information found in my first book, this is a subject that had not entered my mind to write. That is until I heard a popular minister teaching on the subject. While I was awake early one morning, I heard a popular minister teaching on the four gospels of Matthew, Mark, Luke and John. He reached a point to where he was saying that a particular story found in each, was not the same story. This was because of additional information that is given in one of the gospels.

I was immediately shocked because the information in my previous book contradicted his reasoning. However, he pushed my investigation deeper which led to my coming to three conclusions about Judas. It is said that, according to a secular writing, Judas was the son of the brother of Ciapus. This information somewhat confirmed my belief. That as pointed out in Matthew, Mark, Luke and John, Judas was, one, the son of a Pharisee, who, second, happened to be a leper, and, third, would indicate that Judas, himself, was a leper.

The story that is found in all four gospels is the story of the woman and the alabaster box. Most ministers accept the story as recorded in Matthew, Mark and John. They refuse to acknowledge that the story as written in Luke is actually the "icing on the cake" as it relates to the identity of Judas and the religious climate during the time of Jesus.

In my study of these gospels, I found it extremely exciting the way each gospel give important information about this incident that is easily overlooked. Beginning with the first book of the New Testament, Matthew 26:6, it is pointed out that Jesus was in the "house" of Simon the leper. Verse 7 introduces the woman and her actions. When the disciples had "indignation" for the "waste" of the ointment, Jesus pointed out that "... wheresoever this gospel shall be preached in the whole world, there shall also this, that this woman had done, be told for a memorial for her." (Matt26:13).

The overlooked fact about verse 6 is that this "leper" named Simon, maintained a residence in the town of Bethany. Most ministers completely overlook or ignore this point which in itself demands explaination. As pointed out in my previous book, Leviticus 13:12-13 is the test of a leper that is "clean". Based on this law, Simon the "leper" is allowed to live in the town of Bethany where he desired.

The Jews, throughout history, allowed lepers to live within the camp of Israel. I assume that during these times, the lepers had been pronounced clean by the priests. In Numbers 5, is a situation where the Lord required "all" lepers to go outside the camp of Israel. However, after Miriam was made a leper, I feel they were again allowed in the camp (Num 12:10).

In the book of Mark, chapter 14 relates the same incident as being at the house of Simon the leper. The additional information given is the monetary amount which was attached to the actions of the woman. As with Matthew 26:14, Mark 14:10 reports that Judas went unto the chief priests to betray Jesus.

When the incident is related in the book of John, the town is identified as "...Bethany, where Lazarus was which had been dead, whom he raised from the dead.". Lazarus was "one of them" that sat at the table with Jesus. The individual whose home the feast is held at is never mentioned. Although, the instigator of the murmuring against the woman is told. The most important information in John chapter 12:4 is that Judas Iscariot is called "Simons son".

In John 6:71, Judas is called the son of Simon. By chance I was looking through an Amplified Bible at John 6:71 and noticed that it stated ".. .Judas, the son of Simon Iscariot...". From these verses, I began to see that Simon the leper was the father of Judas.

The most compelling piece of information comes from the words of Luke. The book of Luke is the most exciting account of this incident. This is because Luke points out, not that Simon was a leper, but, that he was a Pharisee! This is the point that throws most ministers in to tilt. However, as explained above and in my previous book, lepers could be pronounced "clean" by the priests.

I believe this was the case with Simon the leper. Also, that he was a Pharisee was evidence that the law of Jeroboam, instituted immediately after the time of Solomon was still in full effect. In Luke 7, Luke states that "one of the Pharisees" desired him to eat with him (Luk7:36). Immediately (verse37) the woman with the alabaster box enters.

The minister I mentioned earlier stated this was not the same story of Matthew, Mark and John. This was because the supper was at the house of a Pharisee, and, a Pharisee, according to him, could not be a leper and vice versa. This is further evidence that the law of Jeroboam was still in effect.

Jeroboam instituted the practice of allowing "whomsoever would" to be placed in the service of the priesthood (1Kin13:33). Because his kingdom was not in Jerusalem, he feared losing the people when they went yearly to the temple at Jerusalem. He "took council" but obviously not with the Levites and had two calves of gold made. He placed one in Bethel and the other he put in Dan. His actions are in contrast to Jehoshaphat who about 30 years later "...set judges in the land throughout all the fenced cities of Judah, city by city (2Chr19:5). "Moreover in Jerusalem did Jehoshaphat set of the Levites, and of the priests, and of the chief of the fathers of Israel, for the judgment of the Lord, and for controversies, when they return to Jerusalem." (2Chr19:8). The important thing was that Jehoshaphat returned to using the Levites who had no inheritance in the tribes of Israel. "But the Levites shall do the service of the tabernacle of the congregation, and they shall bear their iniquity: it shall be a statute for ever throughtout your generations, that among the children of Israel, they have no inheritance. But the tithes of the children of Israel, which they offer as an heave offering unto the Lord, I have given to the Levites to inherit: therefore I have said unto them. Among the children of Israel they shall have no inheritance." (Num18:23-24)

However, Jeroboam had commenced the practice of allowing "whomsoever would" to be placed in the service of the priesthood. This practice was subsequently followed by many future leaders of Israel and is believed by this author to have continued through the time of Jesus and today. Further evidence of this fact is when the Pharisee of Luke 7:36 "spake within himself". He reasoned that if Jesus was truely a prophet, he would have known this woman with the alabaster box was a sinner (Luk7:39). Immediately in verse 40, Jesus answers him by calling him by name, "Simon...". If Jesus is in Bethany, and this feast is at the house of Simon the leper, then this "Pharisee" is actually Simon Iscariot, the leper.

As for myself, this is the most conclusive evidence that Simon the leper was a Pharisee. Also, as stated in John, when the home in which the feast was held was not mentioned, the fact that Judas was "Simons son" is compelling evidence. Therefore the information in the four gospels, reveal that Judas was the son of Simon the leper. Also, the Pharisee of Luke chapter 7 was indeed the same Simon.

The critical point is that the practice of allowing "whosoever" to be in positions of leadership continue today. Sadly, many are such that do not fear God (Ex18:21). We Americans have forsaken the laws of God to institute our own laws which contradict the laws of God. In Mark 7:7-9, Jesus made a statement about the practices of his time which are being continued today.

He stated, "Howbeit in vain do they worship me, teaching for doctrines the commandments of men. For laying aside the command of God ye hold the tradition of men as the washing of pots and cups: and many other such like things ye do...Full well ye reject the commandment of God, that ye may keep your own tradition."

As we as a nation continue to allow leaders which have no fear of God to institute laws which contradict the laws of God, our nation deteriorates according to the word of God as proof of Gods existence (Lev18:24-30).

BIBLIOGRAPHY

Almighty God, The Holy Bible

The Constitution of the United States

The Declaration of Independence

The Holy Quran

Proof of God: The True Origin of White People

Taking apart federal budget
(Washingtonpost.com)

Printed in the United States
By Bookmasters